A Biblical Introduction to
THE NEW TESTAMENT

This appears as a paperback edition in the University of Notre Dame Press Contemporary Catechetics Series under the editorial supervision of Josef Goldbrunner.

A Biblical Introduction To
The New Testament

PAUL NEUENZEIT

Translated by
ANNELORE RIEDL

UNIVERSITY OF NOTRE DAME PRESS
Notre Dame

NIHIL OBSTAT:
    Joseph Hoffman, C.S.C.,
    Censor Deputatus

IMPRIMATUR:
    Leo A. Pursley, D.D.,
    Bishop of Fort Wayne-South Bend
    June 15, 1967

Original German title:

KLEINE BIBELKUNDE ZUM NEUEN TESTAMENT
First published by Kosel-Verlag, Munich, 1966

CONTENTS

Contents

ABBREVIATIONS

BZ NF
Biblische Zeitschrift (Paderborn, 1931–1939, 1957 ff.).

Denz.
H. Denzinger/C. Rahner, *Enchiridion Symbolorum* (Barcelona-Freiburg-Rome, 1957).

EB
Enchiridion Biblicum (Naples, Rome, 1954).

ICC
International Critical Commentary (Edinburgh, 1895 ff.).

Kat. Blätter
Katechetische Blätter-Jugendseelsorger (München, 1874 ff.).

LThK
Lexikon für Theologie und Kirche (Freiburg, 1957 ff.).

MüThZ
Theologische Zeitschrift (München, 1950 ff.).

NTD
Das Neue Testament Deutsch (Göttingen, 1932 ff.).

RevScPhilTheol
Revue des sciences philosophiques et théologiques (Paris, 1907 ff.).

RNT   *Regensburger Neues Testament*
             (Regensburg, 1938 ff.).

ZThK   *Zeitschrift für Theologie und
             Kirche* (Tübingen, 1891 ff.).

NOTE: This *Biblical Introduction to the New Testament* is based upon the author's essay entitled "What Is New Testament Exegesis?" in *What Is Theology?* (edited by E. Gossmann and E. Neuhausler [München: Max Hueber Verlag, 1966]). For this edition each chapter has been considerably developed.

I

INTRODUCTION

In recent years we have experienced a remark-
able increase in the publication of new approaches to the study of the Bible. This
revived interest in the sources of Christen-
dom seems to go far beyond the curiosity
of tourists in the dramatic explorations of
scrolls or the archeological discoveries in
Palestine. While this vital interest in the primary sources of Christianity can be found
everywhere, Catholic biblical study in particular is undergoing its first renewal since
the Patristic era of the Church. The development is a rapid one, i.e., epoch-making commentaries on Sacred Scripture written only
ten years ago have already become obsolete
due to the newly gained insights from the
current methods employed in examining
manuscripts, which development of course

has thrown new light on old interpretations. It seems that this new mood of transition and change within theological and ecclesiastical thought has its particular ramifications in all the areas related to Sacred Scripture.

Therefore, it is not merely advisable but indeed urgent that we come to grips with the progression of theological thought and scriptural research. We must digest the results of Old and New Testament studies and transmit them in understandable language to those who in today's classroom and parish church teach and preach the message of God's self-revelation. Hence we need not be disconcerted by the flood of published materials on this subject, which, rather than contradict one another, seem to advance and complete our knowledge of the Scriptures. Moreover, they continue to give us a graphic picture of the untold riches of biblical thought and the limitless number of approaches to the biblical Hebrew mentality, all of which helps to orient and adapt modern thinking and concepts to the foreign world of the Bible. Thus, biblical knowledge depends to a great extent on the state of present-day research in the New Testament and—as far as the catechists are concerned—on the readiness of religious instruction to accept the inspirations offered by the exegetes.

To what extent this has been achieved since the last world war may be concluded by a short survey of the interaction between exegete and catechist since 1945.

In 1943 Catholic biblical research was greatly advanced by Pope Pius XII's encyclical *Divino afflante spiritu.* Catechists welcomed the rediscovery of the importance of the Bible. An important consequence of this new attitude was the appearance of the German *Catholic Catechism,** the first concrete attempt to express theological doctrines by means of biblical concepts and to illustrate the reasons for the faith by means of scriptural texts.[1] If we compare the tendency of Vatican II in its conscientious use of biblical forms of speech in the Conciliar decrees, the "new" catechism in its present style is already somewhat outdated.

In Germany the publication of a Bible textbook for grade schools (*Ecker Bibel, Reich Gottes Bibel*) was another achievement. Here the authors presented a continuous salvation history on the one hand, and on the other

---

* English edition, *The Living Faith* (New York: Herder and Herder).

placed proper stress on the central theological thought so as to throw light on the
kerygma of the message.[2] Thus, "kerygmatic
hermeneutics" was gradually established and
has developed as an independent subject between exegesis and dogmatics. Kerygmatic
hermeneutics aims to create a theoretical
basis for catechetics and to develop specific
methods of reaching specifically "catechetical" conclusions.[3] In the meantime it is important to find ways of conducting a Bible-
catechesis appropriate to the subject matter
and fruitful in its psychological and didactical methods. Protestant catechists have
already contributed valuable proposals and
experiments regarding the application of exegetical scholarship to the classroom situation.[4]

Originally, nearly all biblical texts served
as lessons in the instruction of catechumens,
and thus Old Testament texts were formulated while a rabbi or a teacher of Israel was
instructing the people, or while a prophet
was delivering a sermon.[5] Seldom, if ever,
do we face the fact that the Bible itself is a
catechetical book, a collection of instructive
readings for the catechumens of the early
Church, or, even before that, for the prose-
lytes who would be incorporated into the
chosen people of God. The single texts—

14

which have the characteristics of an address —are not abstract theses or dissertations, but proclamations for those who are to be instructed, much the same as in today's catechesis. Though the designation "catechetics" has a scriptural origin, scholars of today hesitate to use the word in its original sense. Notions from modern anthropology and child psychology have extended its primary meaning of proclaiming "the word of God." Strictly speaking, however, the term "biblical catechesis" is redundant, for the very nature of the interpretation of Scripture seeks to disclose the kerygma of the text. But this fact is no longer self-evident today, since the theological disciplines of exegesis and catechetics have developed in separate ways, and thus need a new synthesis necessitating methodologies of their own. Hence, for instance, St. Paul's careful attempt to guard the Christian message from sliding back into Jewish casuistry is no longer the concern of modern practical biblical catechesis. Perhaps the instructional or pastoral intention of a passage should be considered as a separate problem, a request whose justification is being more and more recognized.

A few years ago it was considered sufficient to transmit to the catechist a picture of the character and origin of Holy Scripture.[6] The modern catechist, however, needs more than this general introduction—he must become part of his proclamation. St. Paul did. His personal polemic against Judaizing elements among the early Christians belongs to the text as a constituent part. Indeed, the individuality of various writers is the only explanation for their differing titles and Christological statements within the New Testament. Hubertus Halbfas justly warns:

> We may be rightly disturbed about the noticeable discrepancy between theological scholarship and the average catechetical practice. Even the most progressive catechetical literature does not attempt a total integration of modern biblical research in interpreting the text. Authors are readily satisfied with making scattered and cautious references to present-day scholarship. Fear often dominates: high school teachers strive to "protect" students from questions which arouse disquiet within themselves; Church authorities consider it enough that a catechist be "pious." [He should not alarm himself by modern exegesis, nor should he be surprised at an occasional, but passing, disturbance in

his faith.] However, neither students nor teachers are "protected" by silencing their common problems; they should learn to face their problems squarely, honestly, and responsibly.[7]

Until now we have been more concerned about psychological readiness and the methods of presentation than about the subject matter itself. We have not really focused our attention upon the vital, compelling problems posed in Sacred Scripture. Because of our mass media of communication, common people are likely to discuss these problems as readily as scholars.[8] (The problems debated at the Vatican II sessions may have aroused an interest among all classes of Christian people.) Care must be taken nevertheless in classrooms and in churches to avoid the stylish tendency of presenting debatable hypotheses as dogmatic facts. The Conciliar instruction concerning the interpretation of the gospels (April 21, 1964)[9] warns us about such unreflected haste; however, this does not mean that an honest question of a catechist should be repressed merely to protect an immature faith. The struggle for a mature Christian self-awareness is everyone's task. Such an effort implies a great love for the Church, fidelity to tradition, and at the same time a courageous search for a contemporary expression of the Christian truths of faith. To this the Council Fathers of Vatican II indeed gave witness.

There is no reason to assume that exegetes are less concerned with the kerygma of scriptural proclamation than are catechists and religious instructors. While their scholarship gives rise to pertinent questions and their methods appear ever more complicated, they are not playing an arbitrary, exegetical game. They are, rather, involved in locating the biblical text within its proper historical context, in freeing the original kerygmatic intent, in making the message comprehensible to a modern Western mentality.

This book aims to give the reader a sensitivity to the exegete's labor in reaching a right understanding of Sacred Scripture and also attempts to open a window into his workshop. It is not the present author's purpose to give practical suggestions for the presentation of biblical subject matter.[10] This comes later for the catechist. Here we are concerned with the first step: that of informing the catechist himself by way of an attempt to determine the point of departure for exegetical works, to familiarize him with the methodology of exegetical research, to define the literary characteristics of New Testament writings, as well as to state the current problems under discussion. While this information alone will not disclose the kerygma of a text, it is a necessary presupposition. It may be called an introduction to exegesis. Generally such introductions are couched in difficult language and are so burdened with detailed, independent questions that the layman finds it hard to get an integrated, overall picture. Besides, the number of popular treatises on the history and literary uniqueness of the Bible has increased. All this published material—presented through a bewildering number of approaches—indicates that it is not sufficient simply to read the Bible; the way into biblical mentality must be opened and paved beforehand. Hence, every catechist whose appointed task is biblical catechesis should have a certain familiarity with the methods of biblical research as part of his background. His knowledge should exceed the tools necessary for the simple lesson, or else he will constantly find himself in a trap.

The following exposition is neither all-inclusive nor original in the treatment of problems. The author's indebtedness to other works becomes evident from the number of references and quotations. These references also show that professional literature need not be wrapped in unintelligible terminology. It is hoped that readers might consult some of these books and make a thorough study of what has been merely indicated here. R. Schnackenburg and others have given a rather complete survey of available introductory material.[11]

Perhaps one day soon someone will do a complete study of the methods of exegesis and the methods of catechesis. Then we may find ourselves analyzing a difficult text or determining its literary form right in a classroom situation. We may then discover to our amazement that some of the exegetical text analyses may be immediately transformed into catechesis, which would contribute to a simplification of biblical instruction and an understanding on the part of the student of the formal qualities of biblical tradition.[12] Again, that is not the purpose of this book, for it is addressed to the catechist. Only if he is convinced of the importance of the biblical testimonies, if he himself has struggled with the dependence of the message upon human and historical conditions, will his instruction be true to biblical attitudes and thinking, will the methods inherent in Scripture itself open up to him.[13]

In summarizing we must say that biblical catechesis is irrelevant without awareness of the basic structural framework of the texts. The exegete offers this knowledge to the catechist. Although, essentially, the objective of the exegete coincides with the objective of the catechist, the exegete's primary concern is to interpret the text, regardless of its didactical usefulness. The catechist, too, should thoroughly inform himself about his subject matter. Modern exegetical scholarship shows that the catechist could make use of the scholarly insights as well as the method of exegesis.[14] This will become feasible only when the catechist knows the methodology and is able to use it to a certain degree, only when he does not shy away from the problems and questions inherent in it and openmindedly attempts to follow the exegete in his biblical research. In the coming chapters we shall try to develop this path, at least in a basic way.

II

MEANING AND FUNCTION
OF BIBLICAL RESEARCH

It is true that Catholic biblical studies are
drawing much attention. Popular books on
the subject (*The Bible Is Right After All,*
etc.) sometimes reach the status of best sellers.
However, it is also true that the biblical student's initial enthusiasm often gives way to
discouragement. Somehow the core of the
message cannot be reached simply by using
a good translation or by consulting an illustrated book about biblical archeology. To the
Catholic Christian, Scripture often remains
the book of seven seals. While he senses the
tremendous importance of the Bible, the layman usually lacks the tools which are necessary in order to approach a truer understanding; he lacks the professional methods
of the exegete. Exegesis often seems sur-
rounded with mystery. Some accuse exegesis

of one-sidedness and a slight tendency toward heresy. Perhaps the propaganda of some biblistic sects has helped to evoke a certain prejudice.

Many church historians, for example, regard with trepidation the recent findings of the Qumran scrolls. Qumran was a Jewish, monastic-like community, separated from the official cult of the Jewish temple. Church historians who are solely set on defending Christianity's unique claim "to save" see this claim threatened by Qumran's "teacher of justice," a salvific figure comparable to the person of Jesus of Nazareth. Exegetes, on the other hand, recognize in these documents a valuable opportunity of gaining insight into the life-sphere of John the Baptist. Such insight, in turn, permits a more concrete description of the milieu out of which and into which Jesus proclaimed his message. Then, too, the writings of Nag Hammadi, discovered near Luxor, Egypt, in 1945, present a rich source of information about Christian and non-Christian gnosis. Here it becomes evident how the Christian message encountered the mentality of the Hellenistic world and how, to make itself heard and comprehended by the people of the Mediterranean area, it struggled to express itself in the words, concepts, and notions of this mentality. The question is whether a message so bound to time and place can really substantiate its claim of salvation after two thousand years. The world of a Caesar Augustus is not our world. During his time various religious trends, myths, cults, and eschatologies were fused into a questionable amalgamation. The images appreciated by this mentality now appear somewhat mythological, unenlightened, academic. On the whole, they do not affect us one way or another. And yet, if the Christian message is meant to be meaningful today, if God has offered salvation to mankind within a historical situation, and if, according to the teaching of the Church, God's word has a binding, obligating character for all times, then nothing may remain undone to make the message intelligible to every new generation. Untiringly we must translate God's offer into the terms of our world structure, the sociological and technological image fit for modern man.

If New Testament exegesis is to measure up to its task, then we must not shun modern methods of literary research. It is neither irreverent nor unbecoming to approach scriptural documents with the same critical scholarship allotted to secular documents of Western thought. Besides turning to the past to investigate the origins of Scripture, exegesis should also turn to the future in an "existential interpretation" which is meaningful to modern man. Although 2 Timothy 3:15–17 makes reference to the Old Testament, it demonstrates at the same time the importance of Scripture for the Christian: "How from childhood you have been acquainted with the sacred writings which are able to instruct you for salvation through faith in Christ Jesus. All Scripture is inspired by God and profitable for teaching, for reproof, for correction and for training in righteousness, that the man of God may be complete, equipped for every good work."

From what has been said, two distinct exegetical approaches become evident. The primary step of the scriptural exegete is to investigate the origins of the writings by means of the critical-historical method. These studies comprise the introduction to Scripture. They involve: a) examining the terminology—text analysis and literary criticism; b) tracing the development of the canon—canonical history; c) investigating the milieu in which the New Testament was written—profane history; and d) discovering the meaning of each verse—exegesis in its strictest sense. The second, the exegete tries to develop an integrated "existential interpretation." Theological subjects, such as pastoral and moral theology, catechetics, and homiletics should of course be encountered from this basis.

III

THE BIBLE AND THE CHURCH

The intrinsic relationship of the Church to Scripture was severed only when the reformers used the latter as an effective weapon against the institutional Church. Sacred Scripture was thereby maneuvered into a position totally foreign to her nature as a teaching instrument and to normal principles of the Church. Earlier, the Church of the third and fourth centuries had specified the presently valid canon of the New Testament from among many elaborate gnostic and apocryphal writings. By selecting these writings in preference to the Patristic tradition, the Church endowed them, and them alone, with the dignity of bearing divine revelation. Only from such a viewpoint and evaluation can we comprehend the origin of the New Testament canon. The Church has

declared Sacred Scripture as her fundamental
law, for which she took responsibility once
and for all. And that is why all theology until
far into the Middle Ages was scriptural theology. The most outstanding theologians, including St. Thomas, wrote comprehensive
commentaries on Sacred Scripture. The origin of the New Testament cannot be thought
of without the living Church; likewise, the
Church, which is removed by generations
from the eye witnesses of Jesus Christ, cannot
be thought of without the documents of this
witness. From these documents, as canons or
rules, the Church orients herself and seeks
guidance for her actions.

Karl Rahner says that the Bible's "normative function for the future Church was exer-
cised precisely by reducing to writing her
paradosis, her faith, her self-construction.
Conversely, her production of the Scriptures
came about precisely as the form in which
she constituted herself the normative law for
her future course. It was by producing the
Scriptures that the apostolic Church gave evidence of the unique power of self-definition
which, as we saw earlier, she needed in order
to be the 'Canon' for the later Church."[1]
We must remember that "the Church's

formal teaching authority and the promised assistance of the Spirit have neither the purpose nor the capability of taking the place of a material norm of Christian faith and morals."[2] Neither disciplinary measures nor decrees inspired by Counter-Reformation resentments and practical considerations may question this canonical character of Scripture.

Progress was made in re-establishing the fundamental relationship between Church and Scripture when Pope Leo XIII founded the Biblical Commission in 1902. Still, the impression remains that some very conventional decisions of the commission retarded, rather than promoted, further research. "In the attempt to guide Catholic biblical research by decree it sometimes made assertions which are untenable in the light of scientifically proven, historical facts."[3]

The Council of Trent formulated the following principle: "Concerning matters of faith and morals, the true meaning of Sacred Scripture is to be considered that which the Church has always held and is holding. The Church alone is given authority to interpret Sacred Scripture, and no one may interpret contrary to this promulgated meaning or proceed counter to the unanimous teaching of the Fathers" (*Denz.* 786). The highly progressive encyclical issued by Pius XII in 1943, *Divino afflante spiritu,* is a defense against too narrow an interpretation of the matters of faith and morals; but the very same encyclical contains a hint that the infallibility of judgments in these concerns should be considered in view of the intention of the historian during his time. Thus, when the Pope restates four times that "our representatives of biblical research should not leave a stone unturned to find what new discoveries were made by archeology, ancient history, and the history of ancient secular literature, so that the intentions of the ancient writers and their way of thinking, narrating, and writing can be comprehended" (*Denz.* 2294, etc.), he does *not* mean that the magisterium of the Church should or would arbitrarily decide about the interpretation of Holy Scripture, especially since Vatican Council I had already presupposed the unanimous teachings of the Fathers or the present-day Church for the interpretations of biblical matters of faith and morals. Such unanimity, however, can rarely be established or proved; hence, the Pope's letter proceeds: "Of the many things contained in Sacred Scripture,

the Church has authoritatively explained
the meaning of very few. Many very important questions remain open for the delibera-
tion and investigation of Catholic exegetes.
Here they should, and are really obligated to,
exercise their scholarly talents in perfect
freedom. . . . This true freedom of the children of God, both loyal to the teaching of the
Church and open to every contribution of
the secular sciences, is the condition and
the source of all true success and permanent
progress of Catholic scholarship." Statements
contained in Vatican II's decree on ecumen-
ism, Article 21, emphasized the importance
of Sacred Scripture in the life of the Church
and appraised with greatest respect Protestant biblical scholarship.[4]

However, it would be a complete misin-
terpretation of the Church's attitude toward
biblical instruction to assume that the
Church disposes of Sacred Scripture at will.
On the contrary, Scripture presents the norm
for the Church.[5] The Church, the immediate norm for our faith, was built upon Scripture, which remains the ultimate norm for
the Church, for our faith, and for theological reflections, exegesis, as well as dogmatics.
"As the word of God, Sacred Scripture carries

31

sovereignty and dignity within itself which does not stem from the Church. The Church merely administers this word as she administers the sacraments. Bound to the word, the Church and her tradition must ever learn anew to listen and obey. The Church is in great need of the pure and true word of God to be cleansed, judged, taught, comforted, and saved."[6]

IV

EXEGESIS, BRANCH OF THEOLOGY

In recent years the position of exegesis within the field of theology has been much discussed. The two opposing points of view had already crystallized in the course of the development of dogma. Until the late Middle Ages there was no doubt that the principal objective of theology was to interpret Sacred Scripture.[1] However, when the reformers, by-passing medieval interpretations of the Church, declared the original text of the Bible as the sole bearer of divine revelation and advocated the exclusive importance of Scripture, the Church began to assume a defensive attitude. In this spirit of Counter-Reformation, Catholic theology relegated Scripture to the background and emphasized instead the speculative aspects of theology, especially apologetics.[2] Thus Catholic theology lost touch with the development of methods in literary research.

Richard Simon, a French priest of the Oratory who died in 1712, may be called the father of modern Catholic exegesis. He attempted to interpret Sacred Scripture by means of the philological and historical methods used to interpret classical texts during the era of Enlightenment. However, Simon failed in his attempt. It was E. Lessing who finally introduced his writings into German Protestant theology. Since neither the efforts of Simon nor any other positive development brought Catholic exegesis to the fore, it remained a purely historical discipline. Thus, theology departments limited Old and New Testament studies to a few semesters. The course was completed before the final and comprehensive examination. Exegesis, like Church history and, in part, fundamental theology, was considered a historical subject, subordinated by far to the apparently more important subjects of systematic theology: dogmatics, canon law, moral and pastoral theology.

Since 1930 this situation has changed drastically. A renewal in Catholic exegesis has caused all other branches of theology to reconsider the primary importance of Sacred Scripture as the source of divine revelation. Perhaps this change was induced by the radical turn within Protestant exegesis, but the encyclical of Pope Pius XII in 1943 also made an impact. Since then an honest effort has been made to establish biblical interpretation as the core of theology with dogmatics as its undisputed crown.[3] Today we say with exegete O. Kuss, "Here, as nowhere else—and only here—we find the truth about divine things and about God himself, because only in Holy Scripture do we deal with the very word of God."[4] However, this absolute claim can be made only if we accept the first principles of exegesis—that God himself has spoken in Sacred Scripture through the human author. This reality is referred to as "inspiration." Then again, the word of God can be grasped only in the literal sense of Sacred Scripture. Since the "word of God has entered completely into the word of man,"[5] the exegete's task consists of taking hold of the exact wordings of the biblical hagiographer. This word of God, in turn, becomes the center and source of all post-apostolic speculations about God, of all *theo-logia*.

Perhaps, in addition to exegetical renewal,

we may cite other causes for re-establishing Sacred Scripture in its central position. Through the ecumenical movement, Catholic scholars became more aware of Protestant exegesis, which had never lost the key position in their theology of being Scripture-centered. The call for *aggiornamento* has also turned our attention back to the sources for the actualization of the Christian message. However, to make these sources intelligible to modern man we need the work of exegesis. The central position of exegesis will finally become an intrinsic necessity; when going beyond historical and philological criticism, exegesis will strive to conceive a theology of the Old and New Testaments.

Reflections of this kind, then, lead to the important question: What, then, is the relationship between exegesis and dogmatics? Since the sources of Christian revelation are historical documents, dogmatics is "unthinkable without exegesis or biblical theology. . . . In fact, Christian exegesis has a critical function to perform with regard to dogmatic hypotheses."[6] On the other hand, exegesis could never arrive at the above made statements concerning revelation by means of its critical-historical method alone. Exegesis

-assumes the Church's pre-understanding of faith. To circumscribe this faith for a contemporary Christian self-awareness is the task of dogmatics and fundamental theology.[7]

Evidently, exegesis and dogmatics depend upon each other and are in need of dialogue. Nor should one of the partners attempt to dislodge the other from its position or overwhelm it. Exegesis alone could not fulfill the task of speculatively penetrating the faith-consciousness of modern man. Nor does dogmatics have the up-to-date methodical tools to approach the biblical text and to interpret it with an awareness of the scientific progress of the age. Therefore dialogue is needed, and not directives or heretical charges. Dogmatists and exegetes must be in sympathy with the problems common to all of us: to alleviate modern man's difficulties in thinking and believing and bring him to a clearer and deeper awareness of the "unfathomable riches of Christ" (Eph 3:8).[8]

V

METHOD OF EXEGESIS

The problem of how to approach the text is a prime point in the discussion among exegetes, dogmatists, and Protestant Scripture scholars. Hermeneutics, as the study of the principles of interpretation is called, has been developed into a special science. It may be considered a branch of fundamental theology. Although Catholic scholars generally agree upon their object of investigation and upon the first principles of theological scholarship, opinions vary on how to handle the texts of Sacred Scripture.[1] Basically, however, Christians of all denominations agree on using the critical-historical method, even though their fundamental postulates may differ one from the other. Some Catholic scholars are hesitant to enter a hermeneutic discussion with Protestant exegetes; some hold the critical-historical method as inadequate because of its relatively recent origin; some fear a disregard for the decisive norm concerning Catholic teaching in matters of faith (*Denz.* 786, 995, 1788).

Perhaps it would be wise to avoid the term "critical method," since it is likely to denote a negative attitude toward Sacred Scripture; it might be better to substitute the term "philological" method. Actually, any purely negative "criticism" would overstep the limits of the method. This could happen if, on the basis of philosophical postulates, those employing the method would declare Sacred Scripture erroneous, regarding it as a mere historical document of a past age: the Old Testament an invention of the Semitic mind and the New Testament a product of the Hellenistic synchronism. Thus, they would reject *a priori* the possibility of miracles and imagine the person of Christ to be a mere faith-construction of the early Christian community.[2]

By critical-historical method we mean, rather, the method developed by the liberal arts during the nineteenth century. This method attempts to clarify the meaning of historical documents through analysis and comparison, distinctions and specifications.

While investigating both the linguistic expression and its historical setting, scholars come closer to the intended meaning of the words. In this scriptural text-analysis, the human power to discern and pass judgment is, above all, confronted with the question of faith and how the text bears witness to this faith. Nevertheless, the dignity of Sacred Scripture demands the same thorough study that scholars expend upon texts of Plato or other classics. "The task of scholarly exegesis consists in using all reasonable means to elicit from the text itself what the authors of the various books intended to communicate."[3]

The exegetical-critical method is also called the "historical method." Since Sacred Scripture was written in the past, it becomes necessary to investigate the conditions under which the texts were conceived and the milieu in which the author lived, his mentality, his level of education, his entire biography. Furthermore, it becomes indispensable to know the structure and the problems of the community to whom these writings were addressed. The objective of Matthew, for instance, addressing a Jewish-Christian community differed essentially from the objective of Luke, addressing non-Jewish converts.

Besides, Luke was a historian steeped in the secular historical sense of his time. Therefore, the attempt to attribute the proper historical place to each text may at times result in a confusing picture. A multitude of dates, facts, incidents, and major events must be considered—a fact which at times gave to exegesis the character of a secret science. To help the neophyte orient himself, experts have provided a vast amount of information, maps, illustrated books on biblical sites, data on customs, introductions to Sacred Scripture, and so on.

Finally, the exegetical-historical method, concerned as it is with the interpretation of manuscripts, needs to be a philological method. The manuscripts under consideration were written in *Koine* Greek, the common man's language in the Mediterranean area at the time of Augustus. *Koine* Greek is simpler and often times smoother than the Classical Greek of Xenophon or Plato; nevertheless, philological problems arise because the Greek of the New Testament was influenced by the Greek translation of the Old Testament. (The *Septuagint* was completed in approximately the second century B.C.) The authors of the New Testament con-

41

tinued the *Septuagint's* efforts to transpose notions of a revealed religion into the common language of the Greeks. To be able to communicate adequately to the Hellenistic world the message of Jesus and the proclamation about Jesus, the Kyrios Christus, the biblical authors at times had to invent new terms. The linguistic task of the exegete, then, consists in tracing the development of terms used in Sacred Scripture, in sensing the nuances of meaning both in single words and in complex notions; he must specify a particular meaning by comparing the wording to similar Old Testament Hebrew terms and terms current in Greek cultic rites or philosophical writings. Any valid statements about what is said in Sacred Scripture require comprehensive grammatical and conceptual research. Conceptual research involves a study of the Semitisms, that is, of figures of speech and syntax originating in the Hebrew, i.e., Semitic language orbit; it results in an understanding of the Hebrew mind. Without a knowledge of these Semitisms, the meaning of many New Testament passages could not be deciphered.

From all this we may not conclude, however, that the exegete absolutely adheres to the literal meaning of each term. "Frequently it is true that a purely logical investigation does not do justice to the inner 'logos' of language. Language is, after all, not a mathematical construction, but a living phenomenon. A true philologist, therefore, will never be satisfied with simply guarding grammatical rules, thinking he could prove the meaning of a text by a mere exact application of rules. Rather, he will become an interpreter; by penetrating the shell of the word, he will try to touch the living thought structure. In this way will he reach the core of what the author had intended to communicate, even if the author was unable to express himself adequately."[4] Thus, philological-historical criticism may be considered the exegete's chief task and his most important tool. By interpreting word for word and verse by verse, he strives to understand the literal sense of a scriptural passage.[5]

In the encyclical *Divino Afflante Spiritu* (*EB* 551), reference is made to the fact that exegetes should strive to determine the literal sense of Scripture. Only through a literal meaning which has been clarified by scholarship can the theological content of various texts be ascertained.

Although the Church has always advocated a reasonable scholarly concern with divine revelation, she has hesitated to approve of this method wholeheartedly. Thus, the task of exegesis as a theological discipline has not been fully defined.

In Scripture we encounter the word of God. It is directed, as in the times of its origin, to the faith of those addressed. It makes a claim, transmits a call, even today. An interpretation which is philologically well analyzed and historically situated attempts thereby to overcome the linguistic and historical breach between the world of Scripture and our world; however, it is still not enough. The entire history of faith and the history of interpretation should be understood, and the free decision-to-faith of each individual believer must be respected. "The true meaning of Scripture, therefore, is not totally determined by precise philological and historical exegesis. In the life of the Church, the meaning of Scripture is also arrived at through pronouncements, decrees, discussions, votes, majority of opinion. Because the message concerns the 'salvation of men,' there is a sort of 'existential exegesis' growing out of the concrete life of the Church as a whole."[6]

With proper precaution we may recognize a certain analogy here to Rudolf Bultmann's so-called existential exegesis, which is based on the postulates of existential philosophy. Bultmann says: "Texts remain dumb without certain presuppositions which stir the capacity to question."[7] Although his postulates differ from those of Catholic exegetes, the principle of necessary presuppositions remains the same. If we admit that science without a preliminary working hypothesis is an impossibility, we may join R. Schnackenburg in saying: "Because of a deep theological conviction, the Catholic exegete *needs* the authoritative interpretation of the Church. Far from making use of this interpretation as a working method to determine the literal sense, this authority serves him as basic hermeneutic principle, as norm and control."[8] His working method, on the other hand, is based on the historical character of biblical revelation. The method best suited to describe the various levels in the process of revelation and the many different literary forms (gospels, letters, epistles, apocalypse, etc.) is the method of philological-historical Bible criticism.

45

VI

OTHER APPROACHES TO SACRED SCRIPTURE

Although the superiority of the critical-historical method cannot be doubted, other theological disciplines make use of divergent methods of interpretation.

The positivistic trend may be termed an extreme of the critical-historical method. The positivistic school strives honestly, though hopelessly, for scientific explanations free from any preconceived notions. It disregards, therefore, the present faith-understanding of the Church and considers Sacred Scripture a mere document of the history of religion, one document among many. Until about 1930 many Protestant exegetes were under the sway of this influence.

The opposite extreme may be called Biblicism. Biblicism regards Sacred Scripture as an indisputably static and given fact with no historical development. The word of Scripture simply stands there to be meditated. Yet, modern man cares little to sacrifice his critical mind for the sake of a naive piety. It is especially important today, therefore, to re-think and reword certain prayer formulations and meditations in the spirit of the biblical renewal. The interest that exegetes show in popularizing Bible readings may be seen in their many magazine articles[1] and popular commentaries.[2] This interest and enthusiasm lead to further questions and a greater demand for explanatory literature about the world of the Bible.

Publications on the subject are legion. Properly speaking, meditations on Sacred Scripture belong in the field of pastoral theology rather than exegesis.

Another approach, the apologetical exegesis, as far as one wants to use it in the former linguistic sense, belongs to fundamental theology. Here, interpretations which are contrary to the teaching of the Church are refuted by means of Sacred Scripture. This is indeed valid. After all, refutation of the first heresies and misunderstandings of the Christian message actually delimited the books of the New Testament. In this way the canon originated. Another matter, however, is the apologetical interpretation during the era of Counter-Reformation already used by the Church Fathers. In the light of the detailed analysis of modern exegesis, this latter apologetical method is no longer feasible.[3]

The so-called *Steinbruch-Exegese* of dogmatic theology is, likewise, outdated. By means of an arbitrarily constructed scriptural mosaic, these dogmatics attempted to prove their speculative tenets by "using Sacred Scripture as building stones for their own edifice."[4]

The uniqueness of dogmatic exegesis consists in a specific interrelationship between the Patristic tradition and the historical development of dogma and canonical decrees. Besides, the dogmatic interpretation seeks the *sensus plenior,* "the deeper or comprehensive meaning intended by God but possibly not definitely intended by the human author. God's intention comes to light only when words, passages, or the content of an entire book are studied in comparison with further revelation or the development of the understanding of revelation."[5] The *sensus plenior,* therefore, cannot be immediately ascertained

from the text. Included in dogmatic interpretation is speculation on how God could
have made his hidden intention known in
the tradition of the Church. But this involves
scientific methods of interpretation which no
longer belong to dogmatic exegesis but to
the field of dogmatics proper.[6]

St. Paul makes much use of typological
exegesis, a method of interpretation which
is based on comparisons. Paul uses the Old
Testament to illustrate persons and events of
the New Testament, pointing out interrelationships in the history of salvation. The
typology of Adam—Christ—(Rom 5) or Abra-
ham, the father of believers (Gal 4), are significant for biblical theology; however, we
should not forget that Paul was interpreting
with apostolic authority and as bearer of
divine revelation. Since typology cannot be
used with the same freedom in post-apostolic
times, we must use caution in approaching
Patristic exegesis, rich in typology, and be
aware of our exegetical limitations. The same
is true of allegory, of which the Fathers of
the Church make ample use and which often
enough changes the entire meaning of a text.
This can no longer claim textual accuracy.
That method is not used today.

We have now sketched the most frequently used methods in the history of interpreting the New Testament. All are more or less valid attempts to unlock the word of God, hidden in the matter of human words, and to speak this word into a contemporary situation. However, we must concede that the method of philological-historical Bible criticism may be considered best suited for a truly scholarly approach to Sacred Scripture. This method respects the Bible as historical document; it also shows awareness of the progressive historical character of divine revelation and the critical, scientific attitude of the modern mentality. Although we may at first regret a devaluation of the imaginative, meditative aspect of an unscholarly exegesis, we may, on the other hand, welcome sober exegesis as a theological discipline of the Catholic Church, a science among the sciences.

VII

INTRODUCTION TO THE
NEW TESTAMENT

In contrast to general or popular introductions to the study of the Bible for lay people, any version of an approach to the New Testament should have a strictly scholarly character. While at first sight it may appear to be merely a preface to exegesis, the scope of its objective will be realized only in actual exegesis. Then the questions concerning traditions, authorship, and so forth are of vital importance. A scholarly introduction, then, investigates the history of texts, the origin of the single books, the history of the canon of the New Testament, and the canonical principles.[1]

TEXTUAL CRITICISM

The authors of the New Testament wrote on pages or scrolls of papyrus. This writing material, made by diagonally pasting one layer of pulp upon another, was not very lasting. Although not a single line of the New Testament has been preserved in the papyrus original, the New Testament documents are generally considered the best-authenticated manuscripts of antiquity. Only a thousandth part of the texts cannot be critically validated, and of those texts relatively few are theologically important. Whereas the first complete manuscript of Homer dates back to the thirteenth century, the two oldest codices of the Bible, written on parchment, go back to the fourth century. They are the *Codex Sinaiticus,* discovered in the monastery of St. Catherine on Mt. Sinai in the year 1844 (which contains the entire New Testament), and the *Codex Vaticanus,* identified in the Vatican Library in 1475. Several papyrus fragments of the New Testament from the second and third centuries have been preserved: page forty-six of the *Chester-Beatty-Papyri* (so called after their English collector) contains nearly all the letters of Paul. The *Papyri Bodmer II and XIV–XV* from the third century contain, in fragments, almost the entire Gospel of John (pages 66 and 75). Another fragment of the same text was found in Egypt. It probably dates back to the year 130. This means that it was copied forty years after the original, a very close proximity.

Of the approximately 2,700 biblical manuscripts handed down to us, seventy are papyrus fragments. We may add to this about 1,600 lectionaries which contain gospel pericopes for reading at liturgical services. Now the wording of these various manuscripts may differ in certain details. The explanation for discrepancies is simple. There were probably mistakes in copying; a tired scribe may have failed to listen attentively during a dictation. Corrections may have been made later on with the intention of adapting the gospel texts or clarifying a concept by means of a comment. An editor may have seen fit to eliminate a grammatical error or stylistic awkwardness. He may have intended to clarify some obscure passage by rewording the whole sentence. Perhaps he wanted to adapt Old Testament quotations to the style of the *Septuagint*.

Another textual source and means of comparison are the scriptural quotations which the Fathers of the Church wove into their writings, as well as the early translations of the Greek New Testament, which appeared in Latin (*Versio Afra* was prepared during the second century in Africa), in the Syriac language (Aramaic dialect, the most important monument, is found in the Bible known as *Peshitta*), in the *Coptic-Hamitic* version, and in many other languages. The achievement of modern textual criticism lies in ordering and systematizing these individual fragments, determining interrelationships and, thereby, judging the authenticity of the manuscripts. As far as it is possible, scholars strive to detect and eliminate deviations. Publications of today, therefore, may be considered nearly identical with the original.[2] Most of these editions make reference to the variables in footnotes, called variants.

Textual criticism has developed a set of principles by which the original version may be ascertained from a number of variables.

1. Generally, the older the manuscript, going back to fewer copying processes, the more trustworthy the text.
2. The more difficult to decipher, the more trustworthy the text, because the tendency of later scribes was to improve the comprehensibility of their predecessor's copy.

3. By the same token, we may assume the
   shorter version to be the original, since
   later scribes attempted to add explanations and comments.

We may not simply assume, however, that
the original text is the one most often mentioned. Deviations may have been passed
from one generation to another. Literary
criticism, far from being a mechanical job,
requires a keen sense of discernment, the
ability to postulate probable causes for deviations that occur. Scholars have set up four
groups of texts:

1. The so-called *Neutral Text* has been verified through the sources *Vaticanus* and
   Sinaiticus as the most trustworthy.
2. The *Western Text* is contained in the
   Codex (D) Bezae or Cantabrigiensis. It
   was used as basis for the Latin translation.
3. The *Textus Receptus* goes back to a Syriac
   text, probably edited by Lucian of Antioch in the third century. During the
   fourth century this was the most commonly used text in the Eastern as well as
   Western Church.
4. The *Alexandrine Text* is represented[3] in
   the *Codex Ephraemi Rescriptus* of the
   fifth century. To this group, too, belong

the Coptic translations which in the year 300 were drastically edited.

Important for present-day scholarship are the *Neutral Text* and the so called *Hesych Text* (signified by the letter H) and the *Koine Text* (signified by the letter K). This latter was exclusively used during antiquity but is less precise than the *Hesych Text*. Although the multiplicity of manuscripts and fragments may appear confusing to the layman, the literary critic strives to obtain a version in agreement with the original text.

CANONICAL HISTORY

The selection of the twenty-seven canonical books rests fundamentally on the principle of inspiration seen from a historical perspective; it represents a three-hundred-year–long process. Throughout this process the early Church delimited the sources of revelation from post-apostolic and nonapostolic writings. During the first three centuries of Christianity the word "canon" stood for what the Church and Christians meant by "inner law," which is the guiding norm of truth, the norm of faith. This sense of canon as an interior norm amalgamated later on with a more formal and static notion meaning "measure, rule, infallible norm," but also "schedule, register." Thus, the Western Church during the fourth century came to understand by "canon" all those apostolic writings which exemplified the norms of the Christian faith. The apostolic preachers could not yet rely on their own Sacred Scriptures. Their concern was to show that in the proclamation of Jesus, the salvific event of his death and resurrection, the Old Testament prophecies had been fulfilled, as the risen Lord explained to his disciples on the way to Emmaus (Lk 24:44–47). The Old Testament law and the writing of the prophets, then, were the Sacred Scriptures which became fulfilled in Jesus Christ. All New Testament writers, however different in their approach, represent the salvific event fulfilled in Christ as the only valid interpretation of the Old Testament (compare 2 Cor 3; 6:15–17). These writers wrote more or less accidentally and not with the expressed intention of receiving canonical acknowledgment in the future. In the early Christian community the person of Christ *is* the canon, the authoritative norm, by which the Old Testament writings are appraised. With his resurrection and ascension the Lord handed his authority to the apostles, entrusting them with the "secrets of the kingdom of God" (Mk 4:11). He invested them with "power and sent them into the world as messengers of his good news" (Mt 28:16–20). The basic structure of the early Christian norm, then, is a tridimensional concept including the *God* of the Old and New Covenants; *Jesus Christ;* and *apostles*. In the writings of Clement (2 *Clem.* 14:2) we find the notion that the apostles are bearers of divine revelation to the same degree as the Old Testament prophets and writers.[4]

Instead of *Christ* as canonical principle, Christians came to think of the *apostles* as canonical principle. But when in the second Christian generation the authoritative proclaimers of the message and the eye and ear witnesses of the death and resurrection of the Lord died, Christians began to collect their writings and to make copies of them. In 2 Peter 3:15 ff., we read for the first time about a collection of Pauline letters. The four gospels were probably compiled in the time of Caesar Hadrian (died 138). Justin knows about them (1 *Apol.* 66 f.; 28; 33) and in liturgical services puts them on a par with

Old Testament prophets. However, during the middle of the second century when Marcion proceeded to repudiate the entire Old Testament, acknowledging only the Gospel of Luke and the ten letters of Paul as New Testament, the Church defended all New Testament writings against heretics, especially against a constantly spreading Christian gnosis. In doing so, the Church prefaced with a prologue the four gospels; the pastoral letters; the Acts; and the Apocalypse. The ten prologues to the letters of Paul were taken from the Marcionistic canon. Around the year 200 the canonical history of the Western Church was provisionally terminated. With the thirty-ninth Easter letter of Athanasius of Alexandria in the year 367 the canon of the Eastern Church, too, was defined. It included twenty-seven books of the New Testament, and it made explicit reference to Apocalypse 22:18 ff., "if anyone adds to them . . . and if anyone takes away from the words. . . ." In the year 405 Pope Innocent I terminated the canon definitively. However, the "Apocalypse" in the Eastern Church and the "Letter to the .Hebrews" in the Western Church remained controversial even in later centuries because their apostolic origin could not be established with certainty.

With this colorful history of the canon we may coordinate the canonical principle according to which the Church declares the New Testament writings as inspired. Inspiration is that charismatic influence of God upon the writer of Sacred Scripture through which, although the writer does not cease to be the literary author, God becomes in a unique way the author of these biblical writings. These writings, then, represent the infallible word of God, the objective norm of faith, for the early Church and for all times.[5]

There seems to be a contradiction between a canonical history where the acceptance of a text as "canonical" develops in time, and the canonical principle which constitutes the text as inspired at the moment of its conception, no matter how accidental the occasion for its production may have been. To resolve this paradox we may distinguish between the fact of inspiration and the Church's reflection upon the fact of inspiration. This problem is very acute in present-day Protestant theology where the inspirational principle is for the most part rejected and a history of a

canon is demanded. The unity of biblical
writings as a basis for an ecumenical theology
is thereby put into question. To establish a
relationship between the fact of inspiration,
the canon, and the Church is the urgent task
of fundamental theology.[6]

SPECIFIC INTRODUCTION

Exegetical problems, which at the present
seem to overthrow some traditional notions
concerning the historicity and authorship of
certain texts, need to be treated in a separate
course of introduction. Since they are of
such tremendous importance, they require
the same explicit presentation as all great
themes of New Testament scholarship.

VIII

GOSPEL RESEARCH

LITERARY CRITICISM

Essentially, all four gospels proclaim the same message: the powerful deeds of Jesus, his suffering and death in Jerusalem, and his resurrection on the third day. Putting aside the Gospel of John for a moment and comparing the three synoptic gospels,[1] we can make these observations:

1. In many texts the synoptics show total agreement.
2. Matthew and Luke share some subject matter unknown to Mark.
3. Matthew and Luke each has specific points not mentioned by the other evangelists.
4. Linguistic and factual research leads us to suppose that in sections where Matthew and Luke agree but deviate extensively

from Mark, changes were imposed by Matthew and Luke upon Mark and not vice versa.

Following these notations we may distinguish the various sources for the synoptic gospels and construct a genealogy:

1. Matthew and Luke based their topographical structure and the sequence of pericopes upon the Greek Gospel of Mark.
2. Besides the Gospel of Mark, Matthew and Luke used another basic source containing a collection of sayings and proverbs.

Although the manuscript as such has not been preserved, we may (because of important discoveries in Nag Hammadi, Egypt, in the year 1945) assume the actual existence of such a collection of Jesus' sayings in the beginning of Christianity. We also find a miscellaneous collection of Jesus' words in the so-called Gospel of Thomas. These sayings are set down incoherently and are strongly influenced by gnostic tendencies. Since Matthew and Luke used the Gospel of Mark and the Source Q (the sayings) as basis for their gospels, the interdependence of the synoptic gospels is often explained by the "theory of two origins." Matthew and Luke do not entirely rely on the sources of Mark and Q, but each makes his unique contribution. We may illustrate this theory by means of a chart.

Specific   Specific
contribution – Mark – Q – contribution of Luke
of Matthew
                    Matthew – Luke

However, the "theory of two origins" is not irrefutable. The *Papias Document,* for instance, contradicts this theory, holding Matthew's to be the oldest gospel. Some Catholic exegetes surmise that Source Q might be identical with this original Hebrew Matthew version. No other hypothesis seems reasonably possible. If we hold the hypothesis of two origins, important insights into the synoptical development may be gained. However, between the death of Jesus and the completion of Mark's Gospel, which is assumed to be the oldest, twenty-five years of oral tradition passed; these need to be thoroughly investigated.

THE HISTORY OF LITERARY FORM AND CRITICISM

Like Jesus, the disciples proclaimed the message of the coming kingdom by word and deed. They also preached the kerygma of the saving event of the death and resurrection of the Lord. When this awaited Second Coming did not occur at the expected time, and the generation of witnesses to his resurrection died out, the need to gather the gospels into a stable and written form became apparent. During the years of oral tradition the gospels had received a definite character which re-appears as a unifying element in all of them. This character was formed during the in-struction of catechumens, in liturgical serv-ices, in a confrontation of the Christian element with a Jewish and pagan milieu. Definite expressions were coined. Under-standably, only configured word-patterns can be transmitted orally over a longer period of time. Jesus himself, in order to make an im-pact on the memory of his listener, made use of word patterns current at his time. The history of literary criticism investigates such word patterns as proverbs, blessings, para-bles, paradigms, words of wisdom, rules for community living, apocalyptic phrases, and "I-words" in which Jesus expresses his own person and his mission. Formal literary criti-cism further investigates the history of the Christian proclamation, its origin, transformations, and traditions. Events, too, were transmitted in word patterns, for instance, in the detailed accounts of miracles such as the storm at sea. To have recognized these word patterns and to have examined the gospels under this formal aspect is the achievement of Martin Dibelius[2] and Rudolf Bultmann,[3] even though in some details their classifications need to be corrected.

The synoptic gospels are not primarily literary works, but written collections of an oral tradition. It is very important for the interpreter to know this. In order to understand a parable, he must know its formal pattern. He must search out the *tertium comparationis* which unites the image and the intended subject matter. Should he attempt to interpret more than the intended meaning, he will miss the essential idea of the parable. In the parable of the workers in the vineyard, for instance, he would fail the idea by questioning the justice of the owner who uses an unfair scale in paying his workers.

A parable differs from a paradigm. The latter is meant to expose the reality communicated in every verse; Mark in the parable of the sower (4:3–8), speaking of the different kinds of ground, presents a paradigm.

An interpretation follows within the gospel (14–20).

The literary forms of the proverb and the story were already known in the rabbinical tradition. Just as the writer of the gospel knew of these literary forms, so the gospel reader of today needs to understand them and the context of their historical setting.

We must remember that the early Christian community had little interest in passing on a biographically exact account and a precise rendering of the words Jesus had spoken. They were too much engaged in solving catechetical problems and in answering the needs of community life. In this process they enriched tradition, thereby adding a newly discovered meaning and developing certain ideas to answer their specific need. Matthew 18 gives us a clear example of such a process. Here the Evangelist presented certain important sayings of the Lord to fit a community situation. This supplementation becomes obvious where the procedure of a fraternal correction is definitely outlined. The offender should face the "tribunal" of the Church. Jesus himself would probably not have spoken of fraternal correction with the same juridical precision (Mt 18:15–17). The words of the Lord, therefore, meet the unique life-situation within the community.

Formal literary criticism, then, attempts to trace the development of Jesus' message during the time of its oral tradition. The objective of the formal critic may never be to extract the pure words of Jesus (*ipsissima vox Jesu*) and present them as *the norm* of the gospels. Rather, through the history of the words of Jesus and their significance in a community, the critic should be able to unfold the first interpretation and Christian practices and, in this way, open up a greater perspective of understanding. We simply do not have immediate access to the precise words of Jesus, but they come to us reflected as it were through the prism of the early Christian community. This fact might have impaired the chronological and topographical accuracy of the sayings but has greatly heightened their color and theological depth. Of course, the historical verification of Jesus' acts and words is very important, lest Christianity become a myth without historical basis; nevertheless, we must be on guard against the tendency of "historicity." In the search for historical detail, this tendency might easily miss the all-important theological meaning. Because the Christian message is not a vague myth containing some salvific notions, modern exegesis attempts to re-examine the relationship of the historical Jesus of Nazareth to the glorified Christ of faith as the early Christian community pro-claimed him and honored him in their litur-gical services. In the gospels the words and deeds of the earthly Jesus are interwoven with praises and confessions of faith in the glorified Kyrios. Although this literary unity may not be dissolved, it may be elucidated for the sake of re-establishing the historical basis of faith.[4]

REDACTIONAL HISTORY

Besides having a basis in both the early Christian community and the historical preaching of Jesus himself, the gospel has a third basis in the theological and community situation of the evangelist. Formal literary criticism considered the evangelist primarily as collector and transmitter of an oral tradi-tion, passing on more or less stable literary forms, making slight redactions in the com-pilation. Redactional historians also consider the frame into which these literary forms were inserted. With the hypothesis of the "theory of two origins" and the formal critical investigation of individual synoptical texts, we now proceed to show *how* Matthew and Luke, for instance, go beyond their pattern of Mark's Gospel and Source Q. Matthew and Luke emphasize one meaning, reduce the importance of another, add a comment, a thematic or literary accent. If we now compare Mark's Gospel with Source Q (both can be hypothetically reconstructed from Matthew and Luke), we may suppose that Mark, too, based his Gospel on a prior tradition. This would mean that Mark already interpreted theologically.

It is fairly well known today how much the discovery of this editorial redactional process has helped to throw primary source material into a new light. If the evangelists were not mere collectors, we may ask what motivated them to edit and interpret the tradition. Was it that they discovered new aspects in the message, that they felt called upon to add their own insights and interpretations? It cannot be said often enough that the preachers of the early Church did not intend merely to pass on the historical facts of the life of Jesus. As witnesses, they wanted to awaken faith in this Jesus. They preached differently to the Jews than to the heathens because of their dissimilar backgrounds. They included their first experiences in community living as well as the liturgy honoring Jesus Christ enthroned at the right hand of the Father.

Since research in this area of redactional history is of recent origin, not many books have been written on the subject.[5] Yet, while the synoptics are not as highly regarded as John or Paul, they may, nevertheless, be counted among the great theologians of the early Church. The characteristics of the synoptic evangelists will in the future be developed into specific theological tracts, for example, Mark the evangelist of the Messianic mystery; Matthew the messenger to and critic of Jewish Christians; Luke the exponent of salvation history and early Christian eschatology and the proclaimer of the social, Christian message.[6]

THE ACTS

Luke illustrates his unique conception of salvation history by the addition of the Acts (which records the time of the early Church) to his Gospel (which records the time of Jesus). Both times are conceived as different epochs of an all-encompassing historical process. These two epochs are distinguished by specific characteristics. On the one hand, Luke looks back to the "arché" of the Church, its uniqueness and irrevocability; on the other hand, he looks ahead to eschatological events. A kind of dual thinking is not, however, the most important aspect of Luke's gospel. His specialty consists in using the content of tradition to represent the entire process of the history of salvation.[7] In recent years the question of Luke's source or tradition has become controversial. Formerly it was common opinion that Luke used the liturgical formulas or creeds exemplified in the *symbolum* (1 Cor 15:3) as a basis for his Acts; now this hypothesis is being questioned.[8] Judging from the book's structure, its entire conception, and its specific Christological aspects, some critics consider it an unequivocal expression of Luke's theology at the end of the first century.[9] On the other hand, Luke gives evidence of the oldest Christology (compare Acts 2:36, 13:33), so that one may rather suspect a combination of tradition and his type of theology. The

Acts may also be considered a witness to apostolic preaching. However, greater attention should be paid to the aspects of Luke's theology. The original apostolic message becomes apparent, not on the surface but on the deeper level.[10]

Although Luke is called the one historian among the evangelists, the principal insight of redactional history still remains true for him. The historical report is subordinated to the theological, kerygmatic content. This does not mean that all factual data lack historical authenticity. Such an assumption would contradict the very sources Luke used as a basis. Yet, the decisive factor lies in the discernment and interpretation of these facts. The themes and the criteria for developing these facts are given by the kerygma of the early Church and the expansion of this Church into the then-known world.

THE JOHANNINE QUESTION

The great gap between the synoptics and the writings of John disappears in the light of recent research in redactional history. Scholars discovered that neither the synoptics nor John write historical reports or biog-

raphies; both present us with a theological
reflection. The Church Fathers had already
called John's Gospel "pneumatic," indicat-
ing that John wrote down insights gained in
meditating the glorified Lord. The synoptic
gospels were called "somatic." Their theological significance was left for this generation to discover. "Now the man who reads
the Bible today cannot rid himself of a certain uncomfortable feeling about this theological manner of historical writing. Doesn't
the evangelist 'bend' the facts to his liking,
distorting the actual events? The facts themselves were partly known to both Jews and
heathens; they were certainly witnessed by
the inner circle of the Church. The facts,
then, were not subjects of discussion. Yet,
these facts were difficult to master, and the
evangelist tried to expound the meaning of
all that had happened. There was the sting
of scandal and embarrassment that needed
to be removed. The evangelists did this with
the means available at their time, and noboby
can say they did not succeed."[11] Above all,
John succeeded in the way he represents the
Passion. With majestic, deeply symbolic language he gives expression to his profound
thought. And strangely enough, compared

to the synoptics, John seems to be even more accurate in mentioning dates and places. He seems to have used early Christian traditions unknown to the others.

The two main problems of Johannine interpretation—authorship and the background of the history of religion—have been thoroughly neglected by Catholic exegetes during the last century. Ever since Rudolf Bultmann[12] wrote his great commentary on the Gospel of John, no one has dared to pick up these complicated questions.[13]

Then there is the question of authorship; we may hold with certainty that the last editors of the Gospel of John, the Letter of John, and the Apocalypse of John are not the same person. To unify the Gospel, the editor probably reworked previous designs and source material before he revised the last editions. While the author of the Letter seems to be of a quiet, balanced, meditative mind producing abstract concepts, the author of the Apocalypse, on the other hand, seems to be a man with passionate feelings and expectations who uses a barbaric form of Greek in spots.[14] Although the oldest ecclesiastical tradition attributes all Johannine writings to the beloved disciple John, this

tradition knows, at the same time, of a pres-
byter named John, in Ephesus, who could be
the author of the Gospel. Furthermore, it is
unlikely that a simple fisherman from Lake
Genesareth should compose such a profound
theological treatise. One hypothesis is that
several primary sources for the Gospel of
John (these have been historically verified)
were collected and edited by a later disciple
of the apostle. It remains nearly certain, however, that the Gospel, the Letter, and the
Apocalypse do not originate from one and
the same author.

More important than the question of
authorship is the historical background out
of which the texts must be understood and
interpreted. The normative, canonical character of revelation cannot be doubted. More
than the synoptics, John seems to be influenced by religious trends and notions out-
side the realm of Old Testament and Christian living. Investigating these trends at the
turn of the century, Catholic scholars fell
into disrepute because of a parallel Protestant development in exegesis. Protestant exegesis had become so liberal that it denounced
a Christian theological autonomy interpreting the Gospel of John exclusively in terms

of the gnostic and Hellenistic culture and religion. Since then it has been established that the Gospel and the Letter of John were composed as a polemic *against* gnostic heresies and other misunderstandings of the message. Although the authors made use of gnostic terminology, they endowed these words with an entirely new meaning.

Until now one could assume the presence of gnostic elements in pre-Christian times, since clear evidence of a gnostic perversion dates only to the second century after Christ. However, the scrolls of Qumran, as well as extended research in the components of Jewish Hellenism, point to pre-Christian gnostic tendencies. The apocryphal Coptic manuscripts of Nag Hammadi show definite gnostic overtones in the manuscript *Veritatis* and the so-called Gospel of Thomas (a collection of sayings of Jesus, comparable to the hypothetical Source Q). At times these elements constitute a complete mythology. "We may, therefore, suppose that the myth of a divine, heavenly being descending to earth, opening the way to the Father by revealing the saving knowledge (gnosis), was widespread before the Gospel of John came into existence. John, then, answered this expectation of a savior to descend from heaven, proclaiming: 'What you are saying has been fulfilled in Jesus of Nazareth. Believe in him!' In doing this, John did not simply adapt the myth or incorporate this gnosis into his writing without modification; he radically reinterpreted the event."[15]

Often we approach the Gospel of John with the wrong questions, unmindful of his unique theological and literary character. Or, we unfairly compare John to the synoptics, crediting the synoptics with a closer proximity to the life of Jesus while ascribing less historical authenticity to John. Nor is it true to say that the Jesus of the synoptic writers addresses the common people, using their short, precise, and proverbial language, while the Jesus of John's Gospel directs his words to scribes and intellectuals. True, in John the theologian outweighs the man who simply transmits a tradition. The great communication about the content of revelation, the dialogues which appear strange to our mode of thinking today, is a way of prophetic proclamation "in which the glorified Lord speaks in the prism of theological reflection."[16] The tremendous significance of the saving act of Christ, of the epiphany of God in his incarnate Son, provides subject matter for ever new and deeper insights. It is the risen Christ seated at the right hand of the Father, and not the pilgrim from Nazareth, who now addresses the liturgical assembly of the faithful through the word. At the end of the first Christian century, John realizes himself to be the mouthpiece of the living Kyrios. Through the Evangelist we hear the word of him who proceeded from the Father and came into the world. Returning to the Father, he still remains with his own. In this characteristic self-revelation of God, John may be considered congenial to Paul. It remains important, however, that the dimension of a lived and experienced theology may not be lost in a hectic search for literary form and probable parallels in the history of religions.

IX

PAUL, HIS PERSON AND HIS WORK

At first sight each of the gospels appears to be a unified whole; the writings of Paul give us this same impression. Further investigation, however, shows the gospels to be very complex pieces of writing. A variety of literary forms and images present themselves. There are independent and dependent statements, interactions between the Jesus-tradition and the kerygma of the risen Lord, and thus many possible reasons for the proclamation of a specific content. Paul's theological train of thought and argumentation may yet be more difficult to understand than the gospel pericopes. The fact that we seldom hear a Sunday sermon about the epistle supports this assumption. On the other hand, Paul has a direct approach, confronting his hearer immediately with the theological insight he wants to present. For instance, Paul does not clothe his words with miracle stories as John does in his sermon on the "Bread of Life." Through and beyond the story, John intends to awaken faith in the Messias. Paul usually addresses a whole community, the nature of which must be painstakingly reconstructed today. Yet, his words have the character of a personal dialogue; he argues and answers individual objections. Paul in his person does not hide behind his words. His personality bears the message.

Paul, like the other evangelists, preaches the gospel of Jesus, the Nazarene, the incarnate Son of God who suffered and died for us on the cross. He reconciled the world with God and in his resurrection won new life for all men. A compendium of Paul's message is presented in 1 Corinthians 15:3 ff. It is the same core message as that of the gospels: Jesus Christ crucified. Paul reflects on the salvation of mankind, the meditation of Christ, on faith and law in the Old Dispensation, freedom and grace, life and death. He presents the scandal of the cross as *the* sign of salvation. Thus, the gospels and the writings of Paul are messages of salvation, each in their unique way of thinking, in their own historical situation addressing their particular groups of people. It seems probable that Paul was aware of the synoptic tradition, although he actually cites the words of Jesus only once or twice. It seems just as probable that the evangelists were not totally ignorant of Pauline theology. Yet, one cannot prove such an interdependence. Really, proof is not necessary in view of the historical character of revelation, opening itself in unique moments and unique human expressions.

The best access to the Pauline writings is the person of Paul himself. In broad outlines his person may be sketched from references in Galatians, 2 Corinthians, and perhaps in Acts 1, although opinions vary as to his origin, education, and so forth.[1]

Paul, born of Jewish parents around the year 10 A.D., was a citizen of the city Tarsus and the Empire of Rome. Raised as a Jew, he grew up bilingually, earning a liberal education. He belonged to the ancestry of Benjamin. From his early youth he confessed a strictly Pharisaical conviction. At the age of twenty, probably after the death of Jesus, Paul went to Jerusalem where he intended to study law. At this time he gathered a noteworthy fund of knowledge about the Old

Testament and rabbinical interpretations. He made frequent references to these in his writings. Undoubtedly, Paul excelled all other apostles in intellectual capacity and actual learning. A decisive hour in Paul's life was his conversion, while he was on his way to persecute the Christians in Damascus. "Paul's metanoia was not a turning away from godlessness and sin to faith in God and the resolution to lead a God-fearing life. It rather pleased this God whom Paul had already served as a Jew to gift him with an unspeakable grace, to reveal his Son to him and to commission him messenger of the gospel."[2] God made Paul a chosen instrument for all heathen nations. Three years later Paul, a Christian, traveled to Peter for the first time. During three mission journeys he had founded a great number of communities in Asia Minor and Greece. In Antioch Paul quarreled with Peter about the freedom of Christians and then also with all the apostles at the Council of Jerusalem, probably in the year 49 or 50. Because of certain clashes with the Jews in Jerusalem, Paul in the year 58 was taken prisoner by the Romans. In the year 60, making use of his Roman citizenship, he came adventurously to Rome. From

83

that time on, the traces of Paul are indefinite. According to tradition, he suffered martyrdom during the persecution of Nero.

"In the polemic of Galatians and 2 Corinthians Paul exhibits his passionate temperament. Unrelentingly, he takes his stand when the purity of Christian teaching is at stake. Without compromise, he fights against those who are Judaizing the gospel. Yet, his character also shows traits of understanding and consideration for the weak. Paul is penetrated by the conviction that an apostle must 'become all things to all men, making himself a slave to all, that he might by all means save some' (1 Cor 9:19–22). His full self-awareness is nothing but an awareness of his mission."[3] This mission-consciousness flows from his personal relationship to Christ. Paul has surrendered himself as servant and steward, so that he can honestly say: "Not I, but Christ lives in me" (Gal 2:20) and "I can do all things in him who strengthens me" (Phil 4:13).

Before beginning to interpret Paul, the exegete should encounter him as a person. Only then will he be able to sense the dialectical tension, the spirit of Pauline theology as a whole. Of course, he must also study the peculiarities of Paul's style, his frequently incoherent thought patterns expressed in anacoluthons and side comments. Whether Paul is more influenced by Jewish-rabbinical or by Hellenistic thought is difficult to answer. Research of recent years has shown that Judaism itself, especially in the Diaspora, was greatly influenced by syncretistic, Hellenistic, and gnostic tendencies. Anyhow, an attempt to systematize the terminology of Paul will fail because the power of his style lies precisely in his incoherent spontaneity.

The reason for Paul's powerful and fluent delivery is his existential motivation. Paul responds to the needs and deficiencies of communities he founded (1 Cor) ; he defines Christian teaching in opposition to heretical tendencies; he corrects a sermon which has been misunderstood; he exposes intrigues among leaders of communities (2 Cor); sometimes he simply introduces himself and communicates his theological creed to a new group of Christians (Rom). Paul recognizes that the only way to salvation, to freedom from sin and death, lies in man's participation in Christ's death and resurrection. In the place of self-perfection through fulfillment of the law, Paul sees the gift of grace through Christ who is the fulfillment of the law (Rom

10:4). Man is justified through faith in him
(Rom 3:22). Baptized in the name of the
Lord, he participates in Christ's death and
resurrection (Rom 6) and becomes a new
creature. This participation in Christ's life
and death is repeatedly intensified in the
Eucharist. The liturgical community becomes the Eucharistic body of Christ, the
Church (1 Cor 11:10). Paul unfolds a new
genealogy in the juxtaposition of Adam,
father of sinful mankind, and Christ, father
of a new generation (Rom 5). Like Adam
who represented all men in sin, Christ represents all men in his act of death and resurrection. (The relationship of those saved to
the act of salvation is thought of today in
terms of a corporate personality.) Also intrinsic to Paul's theology is the Spirit of
Christ, vivifying the community which awaits
the Second Coming of the Lord. In the Spirit
they are able to perform the service and
understand the gifts (1 Cor 12:14). They are
enabled to live a Christian life in responsibility and freedom. Yet, all of this is not
attained without struggle, without the deci-
sion to put away things of the old aeon and
to live in the new. It is the struggle between
the flesh and the spirit.

We have named only a few themes of Pauline theology. A systematic and comprehensive overall view still remains to be articulated by a New Testament theology.[4]

Exegesis of Paul is a difficult problem. Only a few of his letters have been preserved, and absolutely no evidence about the situation of the communities which he addressed has been discovered. The erroneous ways that Paul, in his writings, tried to uproot have to remain hypothetical. We may be certain that in his Letter to the Galatians he carries on a polemic against Judaizing elements. He advocated the Christian freedom from law. The exact nature of the gnostic trends in Corinth has again become a controversial subject in recent years.

The question of authenticity presents another difficulty. We are certain that 1 and 2 Thessalonians, as well as Galatians, 2 Corinthians, Romans, Philippians, and Philemon are authentic Pauline writings. We may also reasonably assume that the two letters to the Corinthians are a compendium of several of Paul's letters to this community. With more precaution we may hold the same about 1 and 2 Thessalonians. The authenticity of Colossians, Ephesians, Philippians, and Philemon may be established and contested with the very same arguments. The letters to the Ephesians and Colossians manifest a development of Paul's Christology and ecclesiology. His doctrine of the Church as the body of Christ, for instance, has undergone a development. A distinction now is made between Christ, the head of the body, and the Church. The Church, in turn, rests upon apostles and prophets; governed by "bishops" and teachers it is a unity of Jews and heathens in the one baptism. This type of ecclesiology is mostly characteristic of Paul's Letter to the Colossians. It is based upon a somewhat gnosticized image of Christ. Furthermore, this letter emphasizes Christ's unique position as sole Mediator and Savior. He represents the reconciliation and fulfillment of the universe. His dominion is above all things. God, acting in Christ, made all cosmic powers powerless. "Under the aspect of reconciliation the cosmic significance of the saving act of Christ becomes especially apparent. How a final reconciliation between the whole world and God will be achieved, remains a difficult speculation."[5]

Undoubtedly Pauline is the Letter to the Philippians, known for its great hymn to

Christ, extolling the degradation and eleva-
tion of the pre-existing God. Equally Pauline
is the private letter to Philemon in which
Paul asks a friend to reaccept his truant slave
as brother to Christ. Because of linguistic,
stylistic, and theological considerations, exegesis doubts the Pauline authorship of Titus
1 and of 2 Timothy. All terminology differs
from that of the main letters of Paul. Besides,
the content is more pragmatic than theological. Here the hierarchical constitution, community rules, ethical behavior patterns, etc.,
are of great importance. These writings
could well present the basis for a theology of
office, for Christian moral attitudes in the
Church and in the world. Their authenticity
in the canonical, inspired sense cannot be
questioned even if it should be proved that
these letters do not originate from the hands
of Paul. They are, nevertheless, an indispensable continuation of Pauline theology, as
well as a necessary practical application of
his doctrine.

Paul may be considered the father of Christian theology. Although a mere fragment of
his oral preaching has been handed down in
writing, and we have no secondary sources
referring to his teaching, he sought to guard

the young Church against defection and re-
version to the mode of a Jewish sect. However,
the teaching of Paul, existentially bound to
his situation, needs to be analyzed. His directives for Christian living, for instance, must
be divorced from the situation of an immi-
nent expectation to the Second Coming if
they are going to be meaningful today. We
must compare Paul's world view with our
own and return to the message with this distinction in mind. "Since Paul was a theologian with his whole being, excluding no
aspect of reality in his religious thought, we
simply cannot separate Paul's theology from
his personality. Exegetes must sense the dyna-
mism of a passionate man in his sometimes
paradoxical statements."[6]

Naming Paul the "Father of Christian
Theology" raises a problem which non-Christian thinkers like to discuss. If Paul played
such an important role in the beginnings of
Christianity, they say, should he not be considered the founder of Christianity? Whereas
Jesus remained in the Jewish realm as the last
prophet of Israel, Paul left Judaism and
"transformed Christianity into a secular syncretistic religion."[7] This discussion goes so
far as to set up an alternative between Jesus

and Paul. This alternative denotes not only two different modes of believing but also two mutually exclusive modes of believing.[8] E. Stauffer asked the pointed question: "Should Paul decide how Jesus ought to be proclaimed in the Church of Jesus Christ?"[9] Paul, they say, made his own theology the exclusive norm of all Christian theology, although it presents an irreconcilable contradiction to the teaching of Jesus. W. G. Kümmel,[10] trying to refute this opinion, compares the total characteristics of Paul's and Jesus' proclamation. Kümmel then traces the historical continuity and the material identity between Paul and Jesus. Kümmel further suggests those points of further study that could yield insight into whether Paul handed down and developed the message of Jesus objectively and truthfully. These points of investigation would be Paul's eschatology, Paul's position within the history of religions, and the meaning and influence Jesus and his word had upon the person of Paul. We may discover that Paul structures his thinking upon the framework of an eschatological scheme of salvation history. Regarding the present time as time of salvation and Christ as the fulfillment of the law, Paul deviates from Palestinian Judaism as well as from Hellenism. "He realizes his dependence upon the kerygma present in the community. The community in turn received this from Jesus himself."[11] Although Paul does not frequently cite the actual words of Jesus, a few references (1 Cor 11:25 ff., 9:14, 7:10) sufficiently transmit the fact that Paul considers the words of Jesus the absolutely final norm. Texts like 1 Thessalonians 1:6, 2 Corinthians 10, and 1 Romans 15:2 ff. can be understood only as references to the earthly life of Jesus, although compared to the Fathers of the Church Paul does not often refer to the synoptic tradition. Kümmel thus summarizes the point of contention:

> Although basically in agreement with Jesus, Paul finds himself confronted with an entirely different situation. Paul as member of the Christian community looks upon the heavenly Kyrios, the glorification of the crucified Jesus. Paul knows of the active presence of his Lord in his community through the Spirit. The reality of salvation, already present and yet proclaimed as the expectation of a coming event, has its roots in Jesus himself. Paul as mere messenger proclaims this reality in a situation newly created by God, the com-

munity situation of the risen Lord. We cannot, therefore, choose between Jesus and Paul. We can only encounter Jesus in the witness of Paul—Jesus, the cause and truth of this witness.[12]

X

HEBREWS; EPISTLES OF JAMES, PETER, JOHN, AND JUDE; APOCALYPSE

These last letters of the New Testament canon never reached the same importance as the gospels or the letters of Paul. Still, we should not underestimate their significance. In a unique way they reflect the theological position and the communal situation of the first post-apostolic generation. They Christianize Jewish and apocalyptic notions. However, exegetes who attempt to prove the historical trustworthiness of these writings run into several difficulties.

The Letter to the Hebrews may be considered the most outstanding of these writings and, next to the Epistle of James, it may boast the most refined Greek usage of the entire New Testament. It is a treatise closely related to Jewish-Hellenistic thought, and it approximates the style of an early Christian homily.[1]

It contains the notion of Christ as high priest and emphasizes the sacrificial aspect of the crucifixion, seeing in the death of Jesus the final termination of the Jewish cult in the temple. This "cultic" aspect represents a new interpretation of the death of Jesus. It may lead us to assume that the Letter to the Hebrews originated in a liturgical context. Furthermore, the idea of a pilgrim-church following Christ in his suffering and his heavenly eschatological fulfillment points toward a Platonic conceptualization.

The seven "Catholic" letters, so called because they were addressed to the whole Church rather than specific communities, received their canonical status much later than the other writings. Theologically fruitful are 1 Peter and 1 John. 1 John is a tract on the basic points of Johannine theology and a warning against heresies. 1 Peter recalls an early Christian baptismal catechesis. It exhorts Christians to be steadfast in faith and in the way of Christian living, even in the face of persecution, because Christ has shed his precious blood in his salvific act of death and resurrection. On the whole, this writing approximates the notions of Paul. Among the directives for specific life-situations, a special exhortation to remain loyal to the secular power of government closely relates to Romans 13. Christ's descent into hell (1 Pet 3:18 ff.) and the exposition of a common priesthood (2:5–10) present the most difficult exegetical problems. 2 Peter shows a literary dependence upon the earlier letter of Jude. The author of 2 Peter (most probably not the same person as the author of 1 Peter) seems to know of a collection of Christian writings, perhaps the letters of Paul. The author of Jude titles himself the "brother of James." He battles against a group of liberal-gnostic pneumatics who think themselves beyond any social order or moral standard and therefore not responsible for any norm of behavior.

The Epistle of James (according to tradition, composed by the Lord's brother James) was dubbed by Luther an "epistle of straw" because of its emphasis upon the works of faith (2:14, "What does it profit a man if he has faith but not works?"). Some scholars claim to detect a Jewish, non-Christian pattern as the basis for this Epistle; in it one finds a series of practical suggestions on how to live. It seems comparable to the proverbs of the Old Testament literature.[2]

The Apocalypse poses yet greater exegetical

problems of authorship and method of interpretation. Should we understand The Apocalypse from the context of persecution, or
should we consider it a suprahistorical theology, concerned with all times? Perhaps these
two aspects cannot be divorced from each
other; certainly, New Testament eschatology
includes the present time as well as the future. Surely, the author of The Apocalypse
does not intend to make prophetic announce-
ments about the history of the Church until
the end of time. Yet, we may call this struggle
to achieve harmony between profane and salvation history the basic theme of the book.
While it may be impossible today to decipher
the language of images, numbers and symbols,
we should not neglect to "develop other fruitful themes, for instance, the image of Christ
in The Apocalypse, the self-understanding
of a persecuted community (Apoc 12), the
thought of martyrdom, the Christian notion
of death, and the contemplation of the coming
kingdom."[3]

XI

NEW TESTAMENT THEOLOGY

The objective of all New Testament scholarship has been the development of a New Testament theology. New Testament theology had its beginning in a nineteenth-century polemic of Catholics against pietistic Protestant orthodoxy. This polemic is no longer relevant. A theology of the New Testament today strives to present the act of revelation in Christ as a unity and as a norm of faith. In contrast to exegesis (which considers authors, themes, literary forms, nuances in language and historical backgrounds, sources, and objectives) New Testament theology wishes to transcend historical conditions. This, of course, requires that exegetical facts and fundamental theological themes of the New Testament be already known. We could not maintain that this basic work of exegesis has been sufficiently done. We can merely point to some methodological examinations[1] and to some inadequate attempts to build up a theology of the New Testament.[2] However, Protestants have produced three theologies of the New Testament. Each approach differs radically from the others in its method and conclusions.[3]

Unquestionably, a New Testament theology is necessary today. Speculative theology, first based upon Greek and later upon Scholastic philosophy, originally used the New Testament only to prove its tenets. Now, although biblical theology expresses itself in Semitic-Hebraic terms, its assertions are no less deep and moving. Moreover, they show greater relevance and conformity to modern thinking.[4]

In distinguishing between dogmatic and biblical theology, C. Spicq says:

> The one attempts to understand revelation with the help of rational philosophy; the other seeks understanding within the documents themselves. While the first makes use of metaphysics and logic, the latter uses philology and history. One argues from a philosophical, the other from a historical point of view. Both, however, agree in

their inspiration and their procedure. Both understand the teaching of the Church as well as the inspired texts themselves in the light of faith.[5]

It is difficult to conceive a practical pattern according to which a New Testament theology could be ordered. Any chronological tracing of theological notions from the time of Jesus' preaching to the Apocalypse turns out to be a noncommital description; it lacks the ability to "call" to faith. Diametrically opposed to this conception, we have the Christocentric concept of salvation history. Its drawback is the tendency to become oversimplified. One could, for instance, regard all divine actions under the unifying motif of agape.

The most satisfactory solution seems to be a combination of all these approaches. After a representation of the various historical positions (community traditions, the synoptics, St. Paul, and St. John), basic themes of the New Testament could be developed.[6] It seems that the object to be represented, the New Testament, demands this kind of procedure. As a historical document, the New Testament contains the various theological fragments in its texts. These fragmentary texts, however, can only be questioned as parts of a directive, canonical norm of the one New Testament witness. New Testament theology transcends pluralistic and fragmentary analysis; it wishes to point toward the truth of the one gospel.[7]

XII

CONCLUSION

Many problems of New Testament exegesis could not even be mentioned here. Many questions that were raised remained unresolved, for instance, the relationship of Jesus of Nazareth to the Christ of proclamation, or the definite design of a New Testament theology. We might have structured our thought upon H. Schlier's question, "What does interpretation mean?" or upon his notion of revelation as history. Some of Schlier's basic thoughts on the subject may be cited.

Here the reasonable interpretation of Sacred Scripture is a significant but painstaking process. It is difficult to understand the meaning of the words of the original texts; it is difficult to translate these unique biblical expressions into modern terms. It is enormously difficult to sense the nature of the writer's involvement, his personal yielding to the call, his assent to its truth. Because this complying to the message has decisive hermeneutic significance, the interpreter, too, must be involved. This constant dialogue in the process of experiencing revelation can be a help to understanding. Our painful efforts to interpret Sacred Scripture must continue, although we may realize that in the last analysis we play a small part in an unending process of clarification. Perhaps we have made God's truth heard more distinctly in our present age, so that it may better serve as rule for and in the world. Who would not want to hear about the promise of a future, about a God of love, who claims the rule of the world in a time of despair and utter uncertainty.[1]

In the above words Schlier has described the effort of exegesis to release God's words into a particular historical time. Because this kind of interpretation asks a response from its listener, it may be called existential, actualizing interpretation. Coupled with the faith-understanding of the Church, the historical-philological method of Bible criticism constitutes the basis for a proper disclosure of scriptural texts.

Pedagogical concerns force us to consider a second step, namely, the translation of biblical scholarship into a practical catechesis. This catechesis should incorporate the genetic structure of specific texts as well as the particular existential character of each pericope. "Modern exegesis points toward an entirely new method of teaching religion. With his catechism in hand, the former catechist did not have to confront biblical texts themselves. This new age, however, necessitates the search for a new approach to biblical didactics."[2] Besides developing the existential interpretation advocated by Bultmann, biblical catechesis needs to develop a methodology specifically adopted to the understanding of children, adolescents, and adults.[3] Perhaps with younger children methods of scholarly exegesis cannot be applied. Paul would say, "Children cannot be fed with solid food, because they are not ready for it" (1 Cor 3:2). However, we may not fall back into a catechetical traditionalism or scrupulosity for fear of scandalizing the "weak." This fear already caused St. Paul to become unsure of himself in deciding about the worship of idols.

Older children, however, must be led to test their faith, rather than to remain asleep

in their half-magical notions of faith. "Often-
times, questions of modern theology which
are interiorly disquieting cannot be resolved
by closing one's eyes and fleeing into a naive
fidelity to the Church."[4] H. Halbfas[5] gives us
an interesting resumé of the opinion of children and young adults concerning the truth
of the Bible and biblical instruction.

They distrust the biblical message because
it demands of them a surrender of their
reasoning power. They hold this sacrifice
of intellect to be an unfair demand. With
a certain sobriety, the majority of youth
expects not to be confronted with a contradiction between a biblical statement and a
scientific view of the world. This youth
simply refuses to accept incompetent instruction which leads to a schizophrenic
self-awareness. Such a crisis of confidence
is caused not by the content of revelation
but by the many misunderstandings of the
officially appointed catechist.

To correct such misunderstandings and to
probe the actuality of revelation must be the
daily task of the catechist. The words of the
Johannine Christ, "The truth will make you
free" (Jn 8:32), may be applied likewise to

those who do research and those who preach. The task may be described in the words of Paul to the Thessalonians, "Test everything; hold fast what is good" (1 Thess 5:22).

NOTES

NOTES TO CHAPTER I

1. Cf. R. Peil, *Handreichung zur Katechese mit dem neuen Katechismus* (Düsseldorf, 1956).

2. Cf. H. Gross, F. Mussner, Chr. Pesch, *Leitfaden zur Katholischen Schulbibel* (Düsseldorf, 1958).

3. T. Kampmann, *Das Geheimnis des Alten Testaments* (München, 1962) 13–32.

4. Cf. B. G. Otto, *Handbuch des Religionsunterrichts* (Hamburg, 1964).

5. I. Baldermann, *Biblische Didaktik* (Hamburg, 1964).

6. P. Neuenzeit, "Gottes Heilshandeln im Neuen Testament," *Im Dienst des Glaubens,* Handbuch zur Missio Canonica, edited by Rocholl-Gärtner (Trier, 1962) I, 113–173.

7. H. Halbfas, *Der Religionsunterricht* (Düsseldorf, 1965) 11.

8. Cf. H. Dallmayr, *Die grossen vier Konzilien* (München, 1961).

9. Instructio de historica Evangeliorum veritate, *BZ NF* 9 (1965) 151–156; cf. R. Schnackenburg, "Zur Auslegung der Heiligen Schrift in unserer Zeit," *Bibel und Leben* 4 (1964) 220–236. See also English translation of the "Instruction on the Historical Truth of the Gospels" in A. Bea,

The Study of the Synoptic Gospels, edited by J. Fitzmyer (New York: Harper & Row, 1965).

10. Cf. H. Halbfas, *Der Bibelunterricht* (Düsseldorf, 1965); A. Läpple, *Biblische Verkündigung in der Zeitenwende,* Werkbuch zur Bibelkatechese, 3 vols. (München, 1964). See also the Insight Series, Paulist Press, 1967, which is an attempt to bridge the gap between theology, especially biblical theology and catechetics, and A. Dulles, *Apologetics and the Biblical Christ* (Westminster, Md.: Newman Press, 1963).

11. R. Schnackenburg, *Neutestamentliche Theologie* (München, 1965) and his essay in J. Scharbert, *Einführung in die Heilige Schrift* (Aschaffenburg, 1961); K. Romaniuk, *Wegweiser in das Neue Testament* (Düsseldorf, 1965); N. Brox, "Einleitung, Einführung, Einübung," *Bibel und Leben* 6 (1965) 223–241. See also R. Schnackenburg, *New Testament Theology Today* (New York: Herder & Herder, 1963), and *Present and Future* (Notre Dame: University of Notre Dame Press, 1966); A. Wikenhauser, *New Testament Introduction* (New York: Herder & Herder, 1958); C. Charlier, *The Christian Approach to the Bible* (Westminster, Md.: Newman Press, 1958); and C. H. Dodd, *The Bible Today* (New York: Macmillan, 1947).

12. P. Neuenzeit, "Die Deutung des Kreuzestodes Jesu," in *Religionspädagogische*

Werkbriefe (1965–66) 6–12, 52–59.

13. Cf. basic works of I. Baldermann, *Biblische Didaktik*.

14. I. Hermann, *Begegnung mit der Bibel* (Düsseldorf, 1964).

NOTES TO CHAPTER III

1. K. Rahner, *Über die Schriftinspiration, Quaestiones disputatae* I (Freiburg, 1958) 56 f.; see also English translation, *Inspiration in the Bible* (New York: Herder and Herder, 1961). Cf. E. Schillebeeckx, "Exegese, Dogmatik und Dogmenentwicklung," in *Exegese und Dogmatik,* edited by H. Vorgrimler (Mainz, 1962) 97.

2. Rahner, *Über die Schriftinspiration* 55.

3. K. H. Schelkle, *Diskussion über die Bibel,* edited by L. Klein (Mainz, 1963) 105; cf. K. Rahner in *Exegese und Dogmatik* 46 ff.

4. Rahner, *Exegese und Dogmatik* 35.

5. Schillebeeckx, "Exegese, Dogmatik . . ." 97.

6. Schelkle, *Diskussion* 106 f.

NOTES TO CHAPTER IV

1. Cf. R. Schnackenburg, "Der Weg der katholischen Exegese," *BZ NF* 2 (1958) 164.

2. Cf. O. Kuss, "Exegese als theologische Aufgabe," *BZ NF* 5 (1961) 176.

3. Cf. G. Söhngen's schema in *Staatslexikon,* vol. 7 (Freiburg, 1962) 968–970.

4. Kuss, "Exegese als theologische Aufgabe" 162.

5. Schnackenburg, "Der Weg der katholischen Exegese" 162.

6. E. Schillebeeckx, "Exegese, Dogmatik und Dogmenentwicklung," in *Exegese und Dogmatik,* edited by H. Vorgrimler (Mainz, 1962) 97; cf. A. Vögtle, "Fortschritt und Problematik der neutestamentlichen Wissenschaft" in *Diskussion über die Bibel* (Mainz, 1963) 67 ff.

7. Cf. K. Rahner in *Exegese und Dogmatik* 28–35.

8. Cf. R. Schnackenburg in *Exegese und Dogmatik* 133; 115ff.

NOTES TO CHAPTER V

1. Cf. R. Schnackenburg, "Der Weg innerhalb der Bibelwissenschaft," *BZ NF* 2 (1958) 169–176; A. Bea, "Biblische Hermeneutik," *LThK* II (1957) 435–439.

2. J. Schmid, "Bibelkritik," *LThK* II (1958) 364 ff.; cf. R. Schnackenburg, "Der Weg der katholischen Exegese," *BZ NF* (1958) 163.

3. R. Schnackenburg, "Der Weg der katholischen Exegese" 162. Cf. bibliography in K. Romaniuk, *Wegweiser in das Neue Testament* (Düsseldorf, 1965) 121 ff.

4. Schnackenburg, "Der Weg der katholischen Exegese" 163 ff.

5. For further references see Romaniuk, *Wegweiser* 20, 25 ff. See also W. D. Davies, *Invi-*

tation to the New Testament (Garden City, N. Y.: Doubleday, 1966); H. C. Kee and F. W. Young, *Understanding the New Testament* (Englewood Cliffs, N. J.: Prentice-Hall, 1957). On the Protestant side, *Kritisch-Exegetischer Kommentar über das Neue Testament,* edited by H. A. W. Meyer (Göttingen, 1832 ff.) 16 parts, latest edition; *Handbuch zum Neuen Testament,* edited by H. Lietzmann and G. Bornekamm (Tübingen, 1960 ff.); *Das Neue Testament Deutsch,* edited by P. Althaus and J. Behm (Göttingen, 1932 ff. [*NTD*]); *The International Critical Commentary on the Holy Scriptures of the Old and New Testament,* edited by S. R. Driver, A. Plummer, and C. A. Briggs (Edinburgh, 1895 ff. [*ICC*]); *The Moffat NT Commentary* (London, 1928 ff.); *Commentaire du Nouveau Testament,* edited by P. Bonnard and O. Cullmann (Neuchâtel/Paris, 1949 ff.).

6. O. Kuss, "Exegese als theologische Aufgabe," *BZ NF* 2 (1958) 172.

7. "Das Problem der Hermeneutik," *ZThK* 47 (1950) 47–69, 62 ff.

8. Schnackenburg, "Der Weg der katholischen Exegese" 172 ff.

NOTES TO CHAPTER VI

1. *Bibel und Leben,* etc. See also Peake's *Commentary on the Bible,* edited by M. Black

and H. H. Rowley (London, New York: T. Nelson, 1962); *The Jerusalem Bible* (Garden City, N. Y.: Doubleday, 1966); and Pamphlet Bible Series, Paulist Press.

2. *Die geistliche Schriftlesung,* etc. See also the following biblical reviews in English: *Bible for Today; Scripture; Catholic Biblical Quarterly.*

3. Cf. J. Michl, "Dogmatischer Schriftbeweis und Exegese," *BZ NF* 2 (1958) 1–14; E. Schillebeeckx and R. Schnackenburg in *Exegese und Dogmatik* (Mainz, 1962).

4. O. Kuss, "Exegese als theologische Aufgabe," *BZ NF* 2 (1958) 178. Cf. R. Schnackenburg in *Exegese und Dogmatik* 115 ff.

5. R. E. Brown, *The Sensus Plenior of Sacred Scripture* (Baltimore, Md.: St. Mary's University, 1955) 92.

6. Cf. R. Schnackenburg, "Der Weg der katholischen Exegese," *BZ NF* 2 (1958) 166; E. Schillebeeckx in *Exegese und Dogmatik* 105–112.

NOTES TO CHAPTER VII

1. The most commonly used commentary on the New Testament is by A. Wikenhauser (Freiburg, 1961). Others: N. Brox, *Bibel und Leben* 6 (1965); K. Romaniuk, *Wegweiser in das Neue Testament* (Düsseldorf, 1965); I. Hermann, *Begegnung mit der*

Bibel (Düsseldorf, 1964); C. Charlier, *Der Christ und die Bibel* (Heidelberg, 1959); U. Wilckens, *Gottes Offenbarung. Ein Weg durch das Neue Testament* (Hamburg, 1963). See also in English: W. D. Davies and Kee-Young (fn 5, chap. 5); C. Charlier (fn 11, chap. 1); A. Robert and A. Feuillet, *Introduction to the New Testament* (New York: Desclée, 1965); and C. H. Dodd, *According to the Scriptures* (London, 1952).

2. Edition of E. Nestle (Stuttgart, 1957); A. Merk (Rome, 1961); H. J. Vogels (Freiburg, 1955).

3. According to Westcott and Hort.

4. Cf. P. Neuenzeit in *Handbuch theologischer Grundbegriffe I,* edited by H. Fries (München, 1962) 781 ff.; N. Appel, *Kanon und Kirche* (Paderborn, 1964). See also articles in J. L. McKenzie, *Dictionary of the Bible* (Milwaukee: Bruce, 1965), and Alan Richardson, *Theological Word Book of the Bible* (New York: Macmillan, 1962).

5. K. Rahner and H. Vorgrimler, *Kleines theologisches Wörterbuch* (Freiburg, 1961) 180 [English translation, *Theological Dictionary* (New York: Herder & Herder, 1965)].

6. Cf. K. Rahner, *Inspiration in the Bible* (New York: Herder & Herder, 1964); E. Flesseman-van Leer, "Prinzipien der Sammlung und Ausscheidung bei der Bildung des Kanons," *ZThK* 61 (1964) 404–420.

NOTES TO CHAPTER VIII

1. *Griechische Synopse:* A. Huck and H. Lietz-
mann (Tübingen, 1950); German edition,
J. Schmid (Regensburg, 1960). See also
Gospel Parallels, edited by Burton H.
Throckmorton (London: T. Nelson, 1949).

2. *Die Formgeschichte des Evangeliums* (Tübingen, 1919, 1959). See also M. Dibelius,
From Tradition to Gospel (London, 1934).

3. *Die Geschichte der synoptischen Tradition*
(Göttingen, 1921, 1958). See also R. Bultmann, *The History of the Synoptic Tradition* (New York: Harper & Row, 1963).

4. Cf. *Der historische Jesus und der kerygma-
tische Christus,* edited by H. Ristow and K.
Matthiae (Berlin, 1964); J. R. Geiselmann,
Die Frage nach dem historischen Jesus
(München, 1965). See also in English: James
M. Robinson, *A New Quest of the Histor-
ical Jesus* (Naperville, Ill.: Allenson, 1959);
J. Peter, *Finding the Historical Jesus* (Lon-
don: Collins, 1965).

5. H. Conzelmann, *Die Mitte der Zeit. Studien
zur Theologie des Lukas* (Tübingen, 1960).
W. Marxsen, *Der Evangelist Markus. Studien zur Redaktionsgeschichte des Evangeliums* (Göttingen, 1959). W. Trilling, *Das
wahre Israel, Studien zur Theologie des
Matthäusevangeliums* (München, 1964); G.
Bornkamm, G. Barth, H. J. Held, *Über-
lieferung und Auslegung im Matthäusevan-
gelium* (Neukirchen, 1963); Also articles by

114

K. Romaniuk, *Wegweiser in das Neue Testament* (Düsseldorf, 1965) 55. In English see also H. Conzelmann, *The Theology of St. Luke* (London: Faber & Faber, 1960); V. Taylor, *The Gospel According to St. Mark* (London: Macmillan, 1952) and *Formation of the Gospel Tradition* (London: Macmillan, 1935); K. Stendhal, *The School of Saint Matthew* (Uppsala, 1954); the Penguin commentaries on the Four Gospels; L. Cerfaux, *The Four Gospels* (Westminster, Md.: Newman Press, 1960); *Faith, Reason and the Gospels,* edited by J. J. Heaney (Westminster, Md.: Newman Press, 1961).

6. See K. Romaniuk, *Wegweiser* 55–76.

7. H. Conzelmann, *Die Mitte der Zeit* 5.

8. M. Dibelius, *Aufsätze zur Apostelgeschichte* (Göttingen, 1961); J. Gewiess, *Die uraposto- lische Heilsverkündigung nach der Apostel- geschichte* (Breslau, 1939); cf. commentaries of E. Haenchen (H. A. W. Meyer, *Komm.* III, Göttingen, 1959) and A. Wikenhauser, *RNT* 5 (Regensburg, 1956). In English see *Studies in the Acts of the Apostles* (New York: Charles Scribner's Sons, 1956); J. Munck, *The Acts of the Apostles* (Garden City, N. Y.: Doubleday, Anchor Bible, 1967).

9. U. Wilckens, *Die Missionsreden der Apos- telgeschichte* (Neukirchen, 1961) 186.

10. R. Schnackenburg, *Neutestamentliche Theo- logie* (München, 1965) 47.

11. K. Romaniuk, *Wegweiser* 76.
12. H. A. W. Meyer, *Kommentar, Das Evangelium des Johannes* (Göttingen 17, 1963).
13. Cf. W. Thüsing, *Die Erhöhung und Verherrlichung Jesu im Johannesevangelium* (Münster, 1960); J. Blank, "Krisis," *Untersuchungen zur johanneischen Christologie und Eschatologie* (Freiburg, 1964); R. Schnackenburg, *Das Johannesevangelium I, Herders theologischer Kommentar zum Neuen Testament* (Freiburg, 1965). See also these English commentaries: C. H. Dodd, *The Interpretation of the Fourth Gospel* (Cambridge, 1955) and *Historical Tradition in the Fourth Gospel* (Cambridge 1963); C. K. Barrett, *The Gospel According to Saint John* (London, S.P.C.K., 1955); and R. E. Brown, *The Gospel According to John* (Garden City, N. Y.: Doubleday, Anchor Bible, 1966).
14. K. Romaniuk, *Wegweiser* 99 ff.
15. *Ibid.* 96.
16. I. Hermann, *Begegnung mit der Bibel* (Düsseldorf, 1964) 84.

NOTES TO CHAPTER IX

1. Cf. B. Rigaux, *Saint Paul et ses Lettres; état de la question* (Bruges: Desclee, 1962); in German, *Paulus und seine Briefe* (München, 1964). E. B. Allo, *Paul, Apôtre de Jesus Christ* (Paris; Cerf, 1942); in German,

Paulus, der Apostel Jesu Christi (Fribourg, 1946). In English: C. Tresmontant, *Saint Paul and the Mystery of Christ* (New York: Harper Torchbooks, 1957); in German, *Paulus in Selbstzeugnissen und Bilddokumenten* (Hamburg, 1959). H. J. Schoeps, *Paulus. Die Theologie des Apostles im Lichte der jüdischen Religionsgeschichte* (Tübingen, 1959); in English, *Paul. The Theology of the Apostle in the Light of Jewish Religious History* (Philadelphia: Westminster Press, 1961). F. W. Maier, *Paulus als Kirchengründer und kirchlicher Organisator* (Würzburg, 1961). K. Romaniuk, *Wegweiser in das Neue Testament* (Düsseldorf, 1965) 102 ff. See also C. H. Dodd, *The Meaning of Paul for Today* (London, Allen & Unwin, 1920); also in Fontana Paperback. J. Blenkinsopp, *Paul's Life in Christ,* Insight Series, Paulist Press, 1967.

2. J. Schmid, article on Paulus, *LThK* VIII (Freiburg, 1963) 216–220.

3. *Ibid.* 218.

4. F. Prat, *"La théologie de S. Paul,"* vol. 2 (Paris, 1949); L. Cerfaux, *Christus in der paulinischen Theologie* (Düsseldorf, 1964). See also in English F. Prat, *The Theology of Saint Paul* (Westminster, Md.: Newman Press, 1952) and L. Cerfaux, *Christ in the Theology of St. Paul* (New York: Herder and Herder, 1959).

5. R. Schnackenburg, *Neutestamentliche Theologie* (München, 1965) 89; cf. F. Mussner, *Christus, das All und die Kirche* (Trier, 1955).

6. R. Schnackenburg, *Neutestamentliche Theologie* 85; cf. O. Kuss, "Die Rolle des Apostels Paulus in der theologischen Entwicklung der Urkirche," *MüThZ* 14 (1963) 1–59, 109–187.

7. W. G. Kümmel, "Jesus und Paulus," *New Testament Studies* 10 (1963–64) 163–181; *Heilsgeschehen und Geschichte* (Marburg, 1965) 440.

8. Martin Buber, *Zwei Glaubensweisen* (Zürich, 1950).

9. *Jesus, Paulus und wir* (Hamburg, 1961).

10. *Ibid.* 447.

11. W. G. Kümmel, "Jesus und Paulus" 450 ff.

12. *Ibid.* 456.

NOTES TO CHAPTER X

1. Cf. F. J. Schierse, *Verheissung und Heilsvollendung* (München, 1955); O. Kuss, "Der theologische Grundgedanke des Hebräerbriefes," *MuThZ* 7 (1956) 233–271, and "Auslegung und Verkündigung," vol. I (Regensburg, 1963) 281–328; R. Schnackenburg, *Neutestamentliche Theologie* (München, 1965) 126 ff. See also commentaries in *The Jerusalem Bible* (Garden City, N. Y.:

Doubleday, 1966) and Peake's commentary
(fn 1, chap. 5).

2. Cf. F. Mussner in *Herders Theol. Kommentar,* vol. XIII, 1 (Freiburg, 1964).

3. Schnackenburg, *Neutestamentliche Theologie* 133.

NOTES TO CHAPTER XI

1. R. Schnackenburg, *Neutestamentliche Theologie* (München, 1965). H. Schlier, "Über Sinn und Aufgabe einer Theologie des Neuen Testaments," *Exegese und Dogmatik* (Mainz, 1962) 69–90; *BZ NF* (1957) 6–23.

2. M. Meinertz, *Theologie des Neuen Testaments,* vol. 2 (Bonn, 1950). See also J. Bonsirven, *Théologie du Nouveau Testament* (Paris, 1951); in English, Bonsirven, *Theology of the New Testament* (Westminster, Md.: Newman Press, 1963).

3. R. Bultmann (Tübingen, 1965); P. Feine (Berlin, 1951); E. Stauffer (Stuttgart, 1948). In English, Bultmann, *Theology of the New Testament* (New York: Kendrick, 1954); Stauffer, *New Testament Theology* (New York: Macmillan, 1956).

4. Schnackenburg, *Neutestamentliche Theologie* 13.

5. "Nouvelles réflexions sur la Théologie Biblique," *RevScPhilTheol* 42 (1958) 209–219,

and "L'avénement de la Theologie Biblique," *ibid.* 35 (1951) 563 ff.

6. Cf. Schnackenburg, *Neutestamentliche Theologie* 18–23.

7. Cf. H. Schlier, *Diskussion über die Bibel*
(Mainz, 1963) 85–98; *Wort und Wahrheit*
19 (1964) 8/9, pp. 504–523. See also Bonsirven's *Theology of the New Testament.*

NOTES TO CHAPTER XII

1. H. Schlier, "Was heisst Auslegung der Heiligen Schrift?" *Wort und Wahrheit* 19
(1964) 8/9, pp. 522 ff.

2. H. Halbfas, *Der Religionsunterricht* (Düsseldorf, 1965) 55.

3. Cf. E. Fuchs, *Hermeneutik* (Bad Cannstatt,
1964) 128 ff.

4. Halbfas, *Der Religionsunterricht* 72–143.

5. *Ibid.* 79–82.